# THE PEARL

by

Kenneth C Steven

Typeset and Published by
The National Poetry Foundation
(Registered Charity No 283032)
27 Mill Road
Fareham
Hants PO16 0TH
(Tel/Fax 01329 822218)

Printed by
Consort Print Services
Consort Court, High Street
Fareham, Hants PO16 7AL
(Tel 01329 822530)

© Kenneth C Steven 1997

Sponsored by Rosemary Arthur

Cover photograph by Campbell R Steven

Photo of author by Richard Campbell, 15 Friarsfield Road, Lanark ML11 9EN. Tel: 01555 663591

Edited by Johnathon Clifford

Poems previously published in *Birds Magazine, Famous Reporter* (Australia), *Good Society Review, Inkshed, Lines Review, Moonstone, Northwords, New Welsh Review, The North, Orbis, Pause, Poetry Wales, Pennine Platform, Poetry Nottingham, Planet, Rustic Rub, Spokes, Staple, Spectrum, West Coast Magazine* and *Weyfarers*.

ISBN 1 900726 05 X

# CONTENTS

**For Simon and Morag,
Jessica and Duncan;
for all the days at Cultullich**

# FRESHWATER

Under the river where dragonflies sizzle all July
And otters turn their sometimes tails like legends
The mussel beds creak, the colour of porcelain, half-hidden
By green trails of weed. Water shepherds come with crooks
Prise up a streaming shell still clasped like steel
And slipping the halves apart, find underneath
A pearl curled fast asleep.

# SEA URCHINS

At the luminous edge of the Hebrides
Where silk water harps the shore
And the beaches are huge boomerangs
Necklaced with seaweed -
They appear, sometimes, curved things
Sharp as hedgehogs, their plates rose
And gold, or even the same green
As Venus at first light. Often
Crusts of waves crack them to pieces
Leave them in jewelled brooches
Up high beside grass and larks.
But each boy dreams of the morning
He looks down on the beach and catches
There at the lips of the water
One unbroken ball rolled
Out of the hand of the sea.

# THE PEARL FISHER

He walked, bent on one side
Like a boat stove in, ribs cracked
Beginning to let in water. The eyes were blue
As a wide bend in a river
A backwater where many-gemmed kingfishers
Flash and thrill. Something had broken him,
Taken the traveller's shoes from his feet
And left him homeless in a village of dry streets,
Waterless talk. Once he'd poled the streams,
Creaked open mussels the colour of lochs,
Found white milk pearls.

But now the string of years was broken
And only a whisky river bled
In grieving from his eyes.

# THE RING

I spoke to him in Gaelic
A few words, like gold dust
Swirled from a Highland river, the last
Of an Eldorado that my grandfather
And his world possessed. It is enough
To make one gold ring about my finger
A marriage to a time that was
The last link before the rivers run dry
And the pure, good water
Stops talking for ever.

# BALRANALD

This place on the edge of living
Shut in by the gales and the whipped water
Broken like sweet cream on the toothless rocks.
Here the birds shuffle along the sand on tiptoe
Rise with weeping into a mouth of wind
And the gulls scream like Viking raiders.
There, out on the last of the eye's journey
Sun coins a golden headland, the sky lights blue
And suddenly the day is made of summer.
Who can translate the curlew's sadness
Into late evening across the moor
A voice as precious as psalms.

# THE LANGUAGE OF THE LAND

Why come back to this poor bit of land
Suffering the worst of the north wind?
The pibroch of curlew at early evening
The lochs like sheepdogs' eyes
Lying flat and ruffled on the moors.
Sudden cottages with their whisky lights
Through the rugged wind of late October.
The tweed hills standing guard on history
Their only kings the eagles' floating gold.

For these reasons I come back here again -
I have not finished translating
Their sadness from Gaelic.

# PERHAPS

Murdo has said it will be a hard winter
He has seen it among the ewes and their lambs
In the blood berries early on the holly.
Perhaps it will be as that year
The house was a snowball in cotton fields
The skies fluffy with falling
And everything stopped: the radios, the cars
The papers, the lights - just that one helicopter
Fluttering over in the late afternoon
Till the farms lit up with lamps that night
The colour of honey. As though we had ridden back
On strange horses into time
When roads were smaller, news was far away
And gifts were precious.
Murdo has said it will be a hard winter -
Perhaps we will journey back to that valley
And find ourselves.

## LOCH LAND

The moor is up to its knees in black water
Midges bundle the grey air, the windless sky
As rain blurs into hills and smudges
A photograph in black and white.

Stumps of men stand like herons by the loch
Looking into a drizzle of mist, pipes
Clamped in their mouths as the rods whip
The bare-backed horses of water.

Nothing here except the prehistoric hills
Like pterodactyls dead and gone to fossil. Only
An otter will bundle overland in early morning
When curlews pipe laments miles away.

Just here the world is dead, a cold moon
Unused since the start of time. Only the fishers
Drum the long track to find this silence
The soundless mouthing of a dying trout.

# BLIZZARD

The fields salted in early morning;
A blizzard at full stretch - its arms flailing
Like a child running home from school.

Lumps of sheep hunched over turnips
The snow slumped against ditches
Drifting in petals through the blind air

And there in nowhere, a string of geese
Like pearls on a broken necklace
Battling north.

# KINCRAIG

A buzzard spun black circles
Disintegrated among trees.

The woods were all the colours of sunlight
Through them the autumn paths chased golden.

The river silted slowly eastwards
Split into a coil of silver eels.

The hills were skulls with vellum skin
In their sockets the lochs lay dead.

Light put a knife of frost on my cheek
At dusk, and drew my blood.

The moon stood white like a barn owl's face
A silken globe in the delicate light.

Somewhere, somewhere within the dark
I heard the wolves of forests ago
Still crying.

# HIGHLAND BULL

He is just an ornament on the moorland
Made of heather roots, too tough for meat
A piece of old machinery with handlebars
Left out to rust in all weathers.

Americans will stop their cars
In a force ten August, iron rain -
Looking for the bull's front end
And a snatched picture.

Yet in him somewhere is an engine room
Quite capable of firing.
Tickle the bracken beast
With care, with a little Gaelic.

# NAPOLEON IN HOSPITAL

There used to be a man
Who came here every week to see his wife.
She didn't know him, just sat resplendent in her chair
Laughing at sudden things inside her head.
Then she'd sit still, her eyes would trace the trees
And watch the birds as though lost childhood
By a pinprick bled into her eyes again.
I used to clean her room, rub the polished floors
Until they smiled once more and smelled of lies.
Her eyes would follow me around
Her mouth triumphant, as though proud history
Had won her fame. I think inside she was Napoleon
Waiting for an army to cut free the exile's chains
March back to glory. Her husband brought supplies
And I, devoted slave, made sure her room was neat
Before the victory. She died a little later
Still giving battle plans in French
To the man who came here every week to see his wife.

# CRANBERRIES

The sky is a single pane of cut blue glass
Under it, the mountains are sharp -
Tents in the north. Below us
The villages wind like blue streams
In the valley's fold. Up above
A hawk flutters in the breeze, a flag
Rippling above a castle of screes
Before folding into a stone and falling
On a flicker of a mouse.
There are cranberries among the heather
Hard bunches, blush red;
We pick them for our Christmas
Four months away from this hillside.

# VOICES

The woodpecker taps out Morse
Crows scrawl arguing across dawn in German.

Woodpigeons make soft French love words
As little twigs of sparrows chatter in Italian.

The raven is Norse, his voice chipped from sharp cliffs
And geese squabble over Icelandic sagas.

In the middle of winter all I hear are the curlews
Crying at night their Gaelic laments.

# THE WINTER BRIDGE

Dead winter. Fifteen geese
Went north in the shape of horns.

The river had stopped talking
Clenched hard as a dead man's fist.

Bronze swords of sun battled the ridges
Legends went by like horses in the mist.

At four the light melted into gold
And a wedding ring of moon
Slipped onto a branch of birch.

# TAWNY

The owl is an old lady with a muffled shawl
Engrained in the shutters of an oak.

She is a patchwork of ancient garments
Sewn together for the moonlit hills.

Her horn-rimmed eyes are always watching
For the moment to glove a mouse.

She glides like a moth from the mist of the trees
And her eyes are of polished glass.

# PLACE

For a little time it is summer.
We have seen the painting
Climbed into its frame and found
The apple trees, the meadow, the old wood house
And a table at noontime.
Afterwards, this canvas, too
Will go into the museum
Where every summer has gone since time began
The place that may only be visited
By the sudden pain of loss.

# THE HOUSEBOAT

Under an awning of willows
Where the river flickers and winks
Where sudden blue splashes of kingfisher
Tip upstream, where the deep beds
Sway jade weed, and the freshwater mussels
Creak and jostle, porcelain blue -
It is there the houseboat lies
Carved out of shadows, low wood
Smelling of cool dark summers spent hidden
From the sun's boiling. It is tethered
By a rope of distant memory
To a place in my childhood.

# EARLY AUTUMN

The cold is a knife, sharpening September trees
With sudden gusts. Dusk smudges the hills
Homes peer out of the mist with honey eyes
Till the rain thrashes back and they vanish
Their lids closed. Rooks topple over the fields
The colour of soot, the scars of their voices
Blown away by the wind.
Along the adders of these roads
Brambles like heavy gemstones
Glimmer wine dark. The river's a white lash
Riding east in a hurry. Our boots belch through the mire
Towards home, to the fires of the night.

# STAGS

The hillsides rust in autumn;
Down them plash glass streams
Knives of cold. Up on long gold shields
Ramparts of mountain, stags strut
Their hides chestnut, heads branched
With proud crowns of horn. Their voices
Are seal howls, echo the weird hollows
These homeless tents of granite stretched
To the sharp blue of evening.
When the snow winters this world
The deer will click closer and closer each day
To the warm, red scent of the house.

# THE GRANDMOTHER

Now I hear her, creaking up above my room
In the still lagoon of morning. Slow she clumps
Across the boards and talks forever to herself
In witches' whispers. I've seen her once
Face like an old onion, the eyes knife slits
And a poor winter of white straw on her head.
No-one goes to see her
She made mischief once and bent her children's lives
With ploughs of guilt. Now she's alone
Cut off by her own blade of hate
From any touch that might have healed her bleeding.

# A POEM FOR IVARS

A picture of Latvia -
You as a boy lifting potatoes behind a horse
Swallows ticking wings in a farmyard sky
The generals of winter a day closer.

In the hungry faces, the simple hands
And this hard road through the furrows of Moscow
I see richer earth still living, wooden songs
That could pull your people's faith.

If a man should come now to your door
Selling motorways, a rustle of money in his eyes
Do not buy his road, for it leads
To all our lost riches, our need of God.

# RUSSIA

One hour forward in time
And thirty years backward
This is the land we feared
Ploughing with horses.

Sad and beautiful tonight
The Neva slipping to the sea
Winter sweeping the streets and whistling
A dance tune from long ago.

Somewhere there is crying
Long and distant
From no-one in the night
But the land beneath.

# CHERNOBYL

In the morning it crackled across the radio
Chernobyl, and a strange yellow light
Filled my mouth with sickness.
That day it rained
We sludged across the moor, shining orange lamps
The oilskins smiling water sheets
Blurs on dead landscape, nothing
But pantaloons of mist, a few crags of deer
Battling away into nowhere. And the rain
Was heavier than ever, and I thought of Noah
And the curved bell of an ark as it came to rest
When the flood was done. But a strange yellow light
Filled my mind that day
Filled my mouth with rain and crying -
It will not be healed again.

# PICKERS

I picked potatoes when the land was waterlogged
All slushed with autumn. An old van bumped us there
The rain came down in curtains; I slumped out
Up to the knees in mud. We huddled a few minutes
While the lungs of the tractor grumbled
And like an insect waddled through the field.

Feet straddled buckets, we lurched on
Until our backs were thorned with pain
A sudden flush of sun came down
I scented blackberries and apple fields far off.

I came home hunchbacked in the evening
A bag of new potatoes dumped downstairs
And a crumpled paper note deep in my pocket -
Pride's first wages.

# LAST JULY

One of those days we were lazy
Went to the coast in a car sticky with July
Windows blowing blue air in our laughter
The fields necklaced with red-roofed farms.
And in the afternoon we sat at cafés
Bare arms leant around our beer, easy
The girls coming past in light swathes, catching
On the rough edges of our eyes.
And in the afternoon we breasted rocky water
Slushed back through the sands, breath shivering
While west of us long oil ships scored the sky
And the sun burst colours slick across the sea.
I never thought of time that night
Or how on separate trains we soon would leave
Those careless days, our young eyes fading.

# THE UMBRELLA DAYS

How we used to quarrel in the rain.
You crying in among red traffic, all alone
Our promises broken
A hub of engines and the smell of faded tempers.

I'd run to catch you up and shine
The rainbow of a smile from your November eyes
And then we'd kiss perhaps, a smudge of make-believe
Left stranded on my cheek. I miss you now
Wherever all the mad umbrella days have gone.

# HALLOWE'EN

Once upon a time our honeyed lanterns
Went in pendulums along these roads;
Faces were haunted with pondweed green
Heads steepled with wizards' hats.

All October the rivers' drums had beaten
Thick to a flashing white. Now late in autumn
The final fires died out among the trees
And bled the land to broken grey.

That night smelled of chestnuts and cold stars
Breath smoked our whispers, groups of witches
Spooked us at corners and howled our backs -
Clattered behind till our chests caught fire.

We rapped at homes along the straggled roads
Sang jaggedly our songs, remembered bits of verse
Then crumbled, broke down in mirth. Yet still we left
With shiver-green apples, copper hands of coins.

Now televisions murder all night long
Their luminous blue tanks light up each window
And no-one anymore will ghost these roads
For Hallowe'en.

# THE SEA CHANGE

I look back into the house
And see the boy who all that barefoot summer
Came inside for sunset, could not sleep
Because June curtains breathed with light.

A blue breeze that was washed in sea
Brought in pale shells and tided morning
He walked through wooden rooms and left
Soft footprints under gulls, the skies' wide shores.

And yet inside these days of endless miles
He cried, and did not know why he should cry
When all the grasses' flowers rubbed his feet
And deep the seas came back to heal his hands.

When now I look at him I think he knew
That childhood broke upon the seas that year
And left sharp spars and masts upon the rocks
And splinters in his eyes.

## THOSE DAYS AND NIGHTS

Corruptly wonderful city
With your chandeliers of churches
Winking over the Neva
Canals sinking through the mist
Archways of trees with April snow
Cars with bad lungs smoking through the streets
Corners selling vodka and women
Huddles of laughter and sweet music
Until with morning leaves of gold the palaces awaken
And Petersburg is older, younger
And green promises bud the wind.

# THE LAST TRAIN

In Trondheim there are rolls and warm milk;
The town is a hum of early cars and voices
Newspapers folded, the blue skies untarnished with cloud.
Outside, the train is waiting, a red the colour of rust
Flocks of children laughing behind windows
Old men criticising the clock, and a few soldiers
With huge thumps of packs on their shoulders
Climbing inside with one easy stride.
Now it is seven thirty, the last cigarettes are stubbed
A few goodbyes hugged on the little platform
And the train begins north, ten hours in its wheels
Forest and mountain and train and forest
Until somewhere the last station stops
And the journey climbs down in the middle of June
And the midnight sun.

# LEARAN

Mid-afternoon and still the light
Blues this silent room. A few dried flowers
Blown out by the cold of winter
Dust the table. And in the window
Trees begin to break with green, their leaves
Uncurl and whisper in an edge of breeze.
This farm lies, a northern shell
A cut of grass between the rubbled Highland rocks
The eyes of lochs that stretch across the west:
It has survived the gales and stands
On wooden crutches looking at the light
Begin to sink. The room falls in on shadow -
One by one our lights ignite the dark.

# THE WARRIOR

And Leif will still bring the sheep to their pens tonight
The moon on his shoulder
His hands chiselled from poorer times
From the mountain legends themselves.
As few words as the snow speaks tonight
He stands out by the blind window, stern like oak
Taut roots unbending, bowed but not brittle
The green sap bending the hunched eyes.

A palisade of stars tonight in western Norway
The gods dance ghosts in the north
Kicking wild flames, laughter of blue-green mouths;
In the morning, he is their ancestor
His stubborn hand will steer the harvest home.

# THE OSLO BOY

I never liked you, Lars
Your voice buzzed with gang fights
There were motorways of scars
Down that city face, you made no bones
About the arms you had broken
The swung jars on drunken faces.

Sometimes, though, a little boy
Only nine or ten crept through that smile
And a good sunset that remembered innocence
Flowed light in your eyes.
Tonight on a train going home
Expelled, the last bell squandered

You are small again and pieces of glass
Breaking in your eyes. Only now, too late
A little fragment cuts my memory
And I see you there, your good foolishness
Trying to grow up so hard.

# THE KITE DAY

The wind has taken us into a wild Atlantic -
Every tree mast's at full creak. Up in the rigging
Birds flutter and blow, keeled by the sudden gusts
That chase them from side to side.

Sudden blunders among the clouds
And sunlight gushes down, drowns the whole valley
In deep primrose. For a moment
The land is still, the trees hold their breath
Before horses of storm clatter back, the rain foams
And the sun's eye blinds.

This is a day for kites
For a boy to struggle the long hill's spine
And feel the paper dragon bumped and bruised
On sharp edges of breeze.

# TRINITY FARM

Somehow the place was evil. No trees sang with birds
The streams were yellow slivers, winking through sedge
Where the gorse watched with cats' eye petals.
Houses crouched on the ground cottages of red-black brick
Fluttering grey flags of smoke. Over this country
The clay sucked down the Roman roads, the broken battles
Till their deaths smelled. Lapwings flopped low over poplars
Weeping for lost causes. Here and there grumbles of tractors
Went in angry humps through broken ground.
Somehow the place was evil. Witchcraft twitched at night
Between the black-wet boughs of alders up to their ankles
In February water. Somewhere a fire kept burning
Strong and bitter; mists would drift across the hillsides
Till the farm was like a lighthouse on an open sea
Set adrift in dusk. And the crow hung upside down against the fence
Swayed in the wind like a warning.

# FIVE DAYS LATER

Only an aeroplane has buzzed across the sky
Slow and unsteady in the butting winds
A midge of a thing, humming towards Glasgow
Islands and seas away.

The war is ended in Yugoslavia
The barricades are gone from Belfast
The blue sapphires of ambulances have stopped
In New York, in London, in Paris.

All that is left is this disinterested silver water
Lipping the stones of the December morning
And a white wind flapping like the last rags
Of an old man's breath.

# FOX

Come upon fox cubs and they're bracken
Tumbling and rubbing in early spring
Where the sun comes down like butter
On a fat fold of the hill.

The fox is quicksand -
A legend in these lost acres of hills
Hung by a brush from the shepherd's wall
Two bangs through the blind head.

# DINGLE

An Irish girl with hair like bracken
Rusting in autumn, and a voice of soft water
Told me of a place she found where dolphins come
Up out of sea the colour of an old wolf
And there is nothing left between there and America.

I am not sure
If it was the truth, or just a story
Mingled with whisky, but it was beautiful
And I put it in my pocket like a pebble
To keep and polish.

# THE WEST

A landscape scoured by ravens
Sudden drifts of rain. The cottages
Pearl black wrecks of basalt
Cry out white and gold in a darkness
Rattled by fists of breeze.
Many weeks the west is delirious
Brave ships buck the sea, their smokes
Smudging a soaked patch of sky.
It is on these days the resin fiddles,
The half-remembered songs are brought
From old hands, passed round with reverence
And voices set on fire with whisky.

# FOX CUB

At the bottom of the field
That yellow-scented morning, first August,
The fox cub, coated in gold and red
Tumbling about among bees and scents
The blackberry eyes watching.

All these years I'd waited
On the dank rim of forests, staring
For a patter of fox, an autumn patch
Out on a dawn patrol. All I heard
Were the gunshot tales of keepers
The banged pride of the foxes
They hung from their walls.

That morning I was the one
Shot by this sudden fox -
The wry slyness of timing.

# PHILIP

In spring, the cherry trees blushed pink
Sudden birds flooded their branches
And the skies opened.

On such mornings I roamed back
Dawn rosing the east, arguments and dreams
Blazing my head.

Your upper room beyond reach
Of the swaying songs all Saturday night
Your room with a guitar, a November fire -
There we began. What threads we webbed
Intricate tales and ideas
Till that dumb pale flame of morning.

All of them washed together
Melted together into one white pearl
Beyond price.